About the Author

Adrienne Brady's career as an English Language and Literature teacher inspired an interest in participating in a master's degree course at Lancaster University. During this time, she won a good number of poetry competitions before taking up overseas teaching positions, where she continued to travel and write travel features for magazines before assembling them into books. The poetry selection is composed of two sections: *From Then till Now*, written while resident in the UK – the second, *Shifting Horizons*, on travels overseas.

Towards the Horizon

Adrienne Brady

Adrienne Brady

Towards the Horizon

Olympia Publishers
London

www.olympiapublishers.com
OLYMPIA PAPERBACK EDITION

A CIP catalogue record for this title is
available from the British Library.

ISBN: 978-1-80439-028-3

This is a work of fiction.
Names, characters, places and incidents originate from the writer's
imagination. Any resemblance to actual persons, living or dead, is
purely coincidental.

First Published in 2024

Olympia Publishers
Tallis House
2 Tallis Street
London
EC4Y 0AB

Printed in Great Britain

Dedication

I dedicate this book to my family: Mark, Catriona, Fiona and Justine.

Life is eternal and love is immortal
and death is only a horizon
and a horizon is nothing save the limit of our sight

—William Penn(1644-1718)

Contents

Towards Winter

Autumn Leaves

See how the leaves cascade about him.
They do not fall in straight lines
Nor land in tidy rows,
Neither do they obey commands.
They are defiant
In their free flight through air
Drifting to the long grass silently.

His extended hands of steel
Pull at the roots of the lawn,
Stab each leaf within arm's reach.
Combed into ordered heaps
They have no voice to speak
Against the unceremonious procession
Towards their funeral pyre.

Controlled at last
Their end seems so complete.
Yet in the fierce beauty of the heat
They are released to fly again:
Unfettered, free, tenuous as the air
Amidst a shower of star

The Wind is Angry

The wind is angry.
He's been in a rage all night
Stamping his feet bellowing
And finally breaking out.
In morning light he gallops
At full tilt round the house,
Charging at the walls,
Pulling at the thatch
And beating with clenched fists
Against the windows.
Even now, he's thrusting
Icy fingers through crevices
And under doors.

The house is tired
And rather bored.
She watches with listless eyes,
Sighs, settles on her haunches
And entrenches herself still more.

Recognition

Between the words
She filled the space
With heavy silence, recognising
That her words did not please.

Between the silence
She filled her heart
With heavy words, recognising
That her silence did not please,

Between the words and the silence
Her thoughts emerged as bubbles
Plasma-red. They grew until,
Recognising the lack of recognition,
They burst and bled.

Volte Face

Yesterday
The ringmaster took me again
To walk the tightrope,
Worn now to a single thread.
He expects obedience.
The children follow my equilibrist role.
I hold the ring to the safety-net,
Watch them fall and bounce upright below.

Today, in full regalia,
Unrecognisable behind his beard,
He's a magician.
He holds his audience spellbound,
Juggles with words and produces
More than rabbits from his hat.
He can make white black.

Off stage the night is dark,
Wind tugs at the guy ropes.
The spotlight falls
Upon the faces of the children.
They believe in magic.
They smile and applaud the show.
The safety net falls, catches shadows.

Scattered Promise

Porpoise-winged creature of the sea
I rise over the waves,
Dive to the ocean's floor
And rise again – a swallow
Resting on currents of air
Lifting and dipping and lifting
Caught in an Arctic flow,
I am snow.

Once I rode on the Severn's
Spring Tide reaching heights
Beyond expectation. I have
Heard the cries of those watching,
I have been their eyes,
I have walked on water,
The sea's edge is where I hide.

I have felt sharp fingers
Trying to prize my shell open,
I am a broken vase
That has been mended before.
I have been a rose
That would not let her petals fall,
I have defied frost.

I have been the shadow
Of the shadow of the moon,
The image in the mirror
That turns its back on the room.
I am sleep beneath wide skies
I am the eyelids of my eyes,
Shutting out the darkness
Beyond the darkness.

I have been the dying
October sun – the drop of blood
From a single sharp prick
Of a thorn – a scarlet poppy
Spilt in a field of corn.
I have been the flag before the bull
Enticing danger – waiting until
It was almost too late before I ran.

I am the thrill of satisfaction
After a kill – a cog in the wheel,
A drawing-pin stuck in the wall
To keep up the wall, the smile
On the face of a clown, a frown
That frightens – a belt that tightens
A serpent, the eyes of a whore
For ever more I am a scattered promise.

M. A.

(Lancaster University)

I have graduated
To this far-flung northern place
To master the art of learning.

You come
From the more familiar south,
Newly-capped and gowned to visit me
Swopping last year's expected
Mother/daughter role.

Together we reach a roundabout
And circle twice,
Choosing a road that leads
To a lift of hills.
Pockets of sun promise gold.

All those years ago
I came upon a roundabout
And spun so fast I lost my way
And felt myself drawn
To an exit I didn't know.

Now I have found the road I missed
And race ahead of you
Dodging the traffic,
A pot of luminous paint
Tight in my hand.

Take the outside lane, my love
And circle, slowly, slowly
See how the signposts shine
Even in the dark.

A Handful of Leaves

Each morning I wake to the sound
Of wind sifting through the oak's
Last brown leaves, like sea
Through shingle. Fingered tips
Of branches scratch careless words
On a blue wash of sky. Below, the day's
Grey sack of letters arrive.

Along a corridor of brown shut doors:
Gary, Andy, Lee – a pint of milk,
'Support C.N.D.' scrawled on torn paper.
Through an open door, a desk lamp's
Naked eye burns beneath a wall of slogans:
After seven weeks, the voice of Stevie Wonder
Still calls to say 'I love you'.

The lift's door opens and closes.
Between floors A and D, the smell
Of cabbage, 'Philip loves Fay',
Cigarette stubs, a red alarm.
Each day I plummet to earth and search
My pigeonhole for your words blue weave
And return with a handful of leaves.

The Sentence

Today we have the sentence. Yesterday
We had parts of speech. Tomorrow
We shall have the paragraph but today,
Today we have the sentence. Seagulls
Fly towards distant horizons
But today we have the sentence.

This is the definite article and this
Is the verb, whose use you will see
When you have been given the subject and this
Is an image which in your case you have not got.
Flowers grow into figures of speech
Which in our case we have not got.

This is the full stop. It is placed here
And shown by a single mark. Please do not let me see
Anyone failing to use it. It must not be used
Until you have completed the sentence. The magnolia
Explodes silently. It never lets anyone see
Its moment of disintegration.

Now we have the adverb. The purpose of this
Is to clarify the action. We can alter
Its position in the sentence. This is called
Sentence construction. Each day the earth's
Position alters. It moves in a circle.
They call it a revolution.

This is a resolution. It is perfectly easy
If you have understood the purpose
And recognise the moment of integration
Which in our case we have not got.
The horizon blurs. The magnolia blossom
Falls. For today we have the sentence.

'Even Amidst Fierce Flame
The Golden Lotus Can Be Planted'
(Inscription on Sylvia Plath's gravestone)

Inexpertly lagged
Against wind-driven snow
We make for the steep track –
Half-river, half-road.

Breath-making, breath
Taking cold prises tears
Of ice. Bare shouldered night
Flaunts a necklace

Of bright, white stones.
The full-blown moon rides
Billowing foam –
A muffled owl cruises.

In the valley below
Amber lights flicker
Like Christmas tree candles.
Hunched and huddled

We follow the moor ridge,
Scurry over cobbles
To the churchyard
As the midnight bells tolls.

Gravestones over-flow to a field
Stiff with frosted grasses.
A torch's golden glow
Halos marble stone.

'Lady, even in fierce cold
Inviolate –
Your memory grows'.

Semantics

Componential Analysis

'a man = human + adult + male'
'a woman = human + adult − male'
'a house, on the other hand, is beyond value'

What worries me
(And it's quite silly, really)
Is what is left of the human and adult me
When the male has been taken away
(I was never good at sums)
I keep asking
But no-one can say

Not liking to know
That I am a partly-missing person
I have decided
(I'm not much good at logic either)
That the next time
I am asked to define myself
I shall say HOUSE

(Quote from 'Semantics: Dr G. Leech')

Published in the Spectator

Almost December

Sun and rain and sun
And a bloom of rainbows –
The sky dissolves again.

The leaf-logged path
To Coniston is a rushing stream.
We jump from rock to rock
Along its sides, balancing
Like goats and sheep – carefully
Over a dead, reclining sheep.

Through a silver spray of birch
The metallic lake breathes out
Its store of summer heat
And shines – we could almost
Picnic on its shores.

The Old Man of Coniston
Has ice-scoured sides –
Head and shoulders in cloud
He is blind to seasons.

Between hill and lake
The slow creep of bracken burns:
Rust-brown, rust gold. Spiked
Black and orange.
Sheep stare and pose.

Up and up into cloud,
Rain ticks on our skin,
Dry-stone walls gleam
Like wet-slate rooftops.
Moorland bog sucks at our feet.

Down and up and down
Through a narrow slit in stones
Where another sheep has died
On its knees, as though resigned
To death – its coat sucked
Between its bones
After the slow decay of flesh.

Fissured valleys leak across
Fields chequered by stone.
We hug ourselves and make our way
Through a mist-wet rush of cloud.

Back across Windermere on this
Almost-dark, almost-December night,
The smooth-black, smooth – slack lake
Heaves, pulls mountains in its wake.

Pre-Christmas News

Some persons have decorated the oak tree
For Christmas – at least, they have tried.
Last night, somewhere between dream and reality
I heard the remains of their festivity rise.

At first light, for one beautiful moment
It seemed as if there had been a surprise
Fall of snow. But snow is discreet and leaves
A delicate tracery of white.

The oak tree looks like a desecrated bride
Clinging to the last shreds of virginity:
Long white streamers criss-cross, loop
And straggle from startled limbs and sides.

It now becomes clear why, over the past weeks,
The supplies of soft white toilet rolls
Have disappeared and why, when I first arrived
At this dedicated seat of learning,

The oak tree had one long strand of white paper –
The non-absorbent type – a remnant of last year's
Decoration, still hanging – like forgotten tinsel
Left on last year's Christmas tree at home.

Towards Spring

After the Solstice

The first day of sun since the solstice.
Leaf absent. Leaf still.
The sky's blue lift is beyond
The topmost, finger-tip touch of branches;
Roots twist leaf-mould deep
Probing far, far into darkness.
A grey colonnade of beech
Is glazed with silver light,
Filigreed branches weave shadows.

Out onto the hill's brow –
Cheek-peppered, breath-curled cold –
Past a century's mushrooming of oak,
Over frost-splintered grass.
The late January lake sleeps deep
Beneath the slow creep of ice
Resisting the sun's thin fire.
We are silent, watching the shift of light,
Hearing bulbs break through earth.

Portfolio

From the photographic display
I remember clearly
Brandt's beautiful woman –
Her half-face, arm and breast
Segmented by shadow.
'Darkness,' you said, 'creates
Its own silhouettes, light lifts
The smooth curves of flesh.'

A clear-cut memory
Framed, like the moments we share.

You, mounting my vagueness,
Quoting Baudelaire and Blake –
Scribbled explanations,
Sketches to illuminate meaning.

You, fast talking, using politics
To blur the edge of my romantic
Leanings – the way your eyes grow
Dark and betray the line of your lips.

A portfolio: stills of light and shade
To outlast the curved and fading edges
Of sepia-tinted days.

Life Still – Blue Model

Dark head to your knees you hug your nakedness
Turn your back on the room.

The artist has contented himself with the play
Of light on your shoulders, the long curve
Of your spine, the line of your head and arm

Resting on one of your drawn up knees.
You are more suggestive and more beautiful
Than any full-frontal woman on canvas

That I know. Are you guarding a terrible secret,
Waiting for the slightest tremor of love
To unfold the petals of yourself?

Or will you, quite suddenly, stand up
And say, 'Why don't you get lost?'
Gesticulate and walk away.

Riddle

I hang on your every word
Compliant yet not all I seem.

My days run in an incomplete circle
That twists and bends towards

A questioned exit. My wardrobe varies
With my changing roll, hanging

In fluid lines that ebb and flow
In shifting light, like crimson

Taffeta shot with green,
Till darkness blends the two.

Now daylight shows my garb is plain
And neat, my mind channelled

To the day. High heels click precision,
My face a mask that melts away.

Needing only space to breathe
I disrobe, becoming pliant,

Bending to your need. When the air
Is tinged with ice I freeze,

Sparkle enticingly – my rigid frame
Not yielding to your touch.

Geocolloid

Easter recess: the university bar
Invaded by police inspectors
And scientific dons, is extended.

We identify moustached inspectors:
Chins clean-shaven – hair neatly cut
Back and sides, sober in dress.
They shift weight from heels to toes,
Sift information with their eyes.
Bespectacled dons, bearded and cerebral,
Wear round-shouldered Aran sweaters,
Search for others of their kind.

One, mistaking my interest
In his conference label asked:
'Are you a geocolloid?' My untruthful
Affirmative reply delighted him.
'Heavens!' he cried, squeezing to my
Side. 'They're usually bearded
and bald.' Under closer examination
My faltering replies exposed deception.

The next night at the bar,
Between the police inspectors
He confessed that he'd remember
The conference best for the girl –
Thinly disguised – who arrested his attention.
He raised his glass, professed
His verdict. Was concise:
'Honorary geocolloid for life.'

You Ain't Seen Nothing Yet!

Ladies and gentlemen, this way
For the main attraction: a Bikini display
Of such magnificent proportions
You won't believe your eyes:
The setting, a perfect Pacific
Blue backdrop of ocean –

A Micronesian coral island
Where all dreams come true.
Step aboard Operation Crossroads;
Journalists and photographers
This way – this is your day too
For the scoop of the century.

The voyage is over –
Your destination is here
On this paradisal island.
The stage has been set
Alongside a sleepy lagoon
Where nature is undisturbed

And no expense has been spared
For the treat in store for you.
This vast armada of workers
And onlookers is beyond compare
With that of any spectacle
Seen anywhere before this day.

Take your seats please,
Count down is near – remember
To keep your eyes pared;
It will last but a moment.
You might say it's a long way
To come for such brief exposure
But it's the afterglow that's rare.
Prepare for that action-packed
fraction of a second –
Such satisfaction is guaranteed
To last more than a lifetime.
Look towards Kwajalein

Where Dave's Dream carries Gilda
The girl of the day –
See, a new star is born
Low on the distant horizon.
Watch as she swells and grows
Becoming more alluring,

Brighter by the second
Till she penetrates the dark lens
Of the eye filling the mind.
See how her magical display
Takes shape, filling like a huge
Balloon that grows into the dome

Of a mosque in a dream.
Feel her life throbbing:
A giant pulse generating
More heat than the sun itself.
Now she changes shape again
Forming a mushroom cloud

Of amazing size in minutes alone,
Then stripping she disappears
Before your very eyes.
See how the ocean leaps towards
The skies applauding the show.
Feel the aftermath glow.

Ladies and gentlemen, don't go
– You have seen nothing yet!
What you have witnessed this day
Is no more than a matchstick,
The simple detonator
Of what we have in store.
Buy your tickets now for the next display.

(*U.S.A. nuclear testing site: Bikini Atoll, Kwajalein*)

Tax-Free

April in Belgrave Square. It snows.
Inside closed doors a security guard
Speaks Arabic into a radio on his chest,
From his upholstered hips – a dark
Metallic glow. A plaque commemorates
Churchill's ministerial post.

'An interview? The university?'
I reply to question – mark eyes
Behind a polished desk and make
My way over crushed-grape carpet
To a bilingual basement below. Walls
Surprise with posters: Arab stallions,
Minarets, cerulian skies, cloud-free.

My assessor smokes and notes
In red biro, my research and publications.
'My salary – his eyes rest on my knees –
The figure you state is after tax?'
'The Kingdom,' he says
'Is generous – you will be free from tax.'

My white Suzuki
Seeks sun-dust desert roads, past
Moorish temples, melting sugar domes
To the mountains and lakes of Abha.
I'll visit Joan in Sana and maybe…

He breaks my reverie –
'You have some questions?'
'My car, shall I take it with me?'
'That cannot be' – indelible marble eyes.
'It's not permitted for women to drive.'

Don't rise. Don't show a trace
Of what's inside. An acquiescent smile
Will please. When the contract's
Signed and sealed, your heels walking
Walking, walking – tax-free
Then the time may be right
To bite the hand that feeds.

Portrait

The morning sun comes in, goes out
At the flick of a switch.
The seasons flurry, a swirl of dried leaves,
A stirring of tightly budded tips.
The sky is blue – is white – is black.

A shot through trees to the river:
Each outstretched twig holds a quiver
Of light, weaves a silver web between
Water and sky, intangible as a rainbow.

A man is standing midstream,
Calling his dogs. They come on tiptoe,
For the cold, tails between their legs.
She focuses her camera. He smiles,
Removes his glasses. She clicks.

Over The Edge

They cross the moor ridge and go
Headfirst into the valley. Half-way down
Where grass thins and dark trees begin
The track curves, a curl of smoke

Welcomes them – black stone set in black.
The place is unchanged.
The opposite hill charred from a fire
Some five years back still leans this way.

The valley gapes: a woman in labour,
Legs splayed, indifferent to onlookers.
Breasts that would be small and soft
Are mountains of granite, blue-veined.

The slate – blue sky turns indigo,
Logs shift and hiss in the grate.
Over tea and ginger cake
They become again a part of the place.

She fixes her eyes on his face, remembers
That when she was skiing she had seen
That shadows on snow were blue,
White mountains open.

A Camille Pissario evening
Dissolves from blue to grey.
In the darkness beyond, birthwaters
Trickle away. Somewhere, out of sight

A dragon lies in wait, its threshing tail
Has dragged stars from the sky.
They lie in the valley, glitter at the head.
Firelight flickers. A circle of grey figures

Cling to the walls – too tall they lean
And sway as heavy headed roses, to listen.
A wine cork implodes, sprays the ceiling red.
She runs her finger round the rim of the glass

Feels the music's edge – the slow spin…
The house sleeps. A grey wash of sky through
Slatted lids, the scent of hyacinths. Soon the
Tightly-sheathed magnolia will ignite the morning.

Going on Sunday

Saturday night – going on Sunday
We hesitate in a swirl of snow then
Make for the craziest place in town.

Through black doors etched with gold:
A honeycomb of alcoves, a haze of smoke,
Music to cancel conversation.

Averaging about five-feet-five,
Furtive-eyed males bulge tightly
In corners, drinking and watching

Girls not destined for lining walls.
Magazine-faced, they glow
Over Monroe clinging silks, swing

Global hips, dance stiletto-jigs
Between a litter of handbags.
They are the lustre of their dreams.

Madonna sings like a virgin,
Couples fondle, men dance: man to man.
Underdressed and overage, careless

Of partners and the onlooker's gaze,
We leave cool glasses of lime
And dry white wine to dance and pray:

Dear God, keep the lights low, play us
Some sixties music and send us six feet
Of Robert Redford or Michael Caine.

Christmas at Easter

(Monte Bondone, Italy)

Easter Sunday evening
In failing light and falling snow
Our boots crunch uphill munching
Their way from the Hotel Grenzienella
To the tiny Alpine church
Lost among tall firs on Monte Bondone.

Passing the neighbouring hotel
Resurrects memories – still warm –
Of last night's late disco.
We are watched, wanted by dark eyed Italians
Waiting in the shadows of the cellar's pillars.
Invitations to dance are invitations to love.

Bands of gold bar no hold here
– beneath our feet squares of light flare
In technicoloured frenzy, bodies rise and fall
On a sea of sound. Cinderella-like
We break from the heat into the white, light night
And tumble through the snow, laughing.

Further uphill is Chico's Pizzeria;
We remember his bespectacled kindness
– Watching us count our dwindling lire,
Eating wafer-thin pizzas, accepting his gift
Of flowers – parting kisses still linger.

Now bells ring and soft flakes
Settle on our lashes – translucent tears.
Peopled by shadows the mountains sing
Their silent hosannas; bearing our grief
And shaking snow from us we enter the church
Amidst a mass of strangers.
Familiar words in an unfamiliar tongue
Spill outside into the cold:
For those for whom there was no room,
For those who did not come.
Through the darkening window a giant fir upholds
Weighted branches: a crucifix against the snow.

A Mile High

Above the clouds
Somewhere between Ljubljana and Heathrow
He invited me to join the Mile High Club.
Our feet had not touched ground all week –
An intimacy of strangers a mile and a half high
In Kranjska Gora's frost-held crystal bowl.

Dressed unisex-style in streamlined, bright clothes
We drank deep draughts of cold rarefied air,
Viewed the strange, white world through
Wide-angled lens, saw skies tinted rose,
Slopes veined indigo, flew on winged feet
Through heavily laden firs over a rush of snow

To the mountain's very peak. In an ecstasy
Of cinnamon and cloves we sip hot wine,
Tumble in deep soft folds. Black-moustached
Pedro's quick dance led us over hidden
Tongues of ice into the falling mile-high-night,
Moonboot deep in snow.

Towards Summer

A Gathering of Swallows

Easter: like migratory birds
The children return from their winter haunts.
Last year it was a different place:
A sweep of lawn fringed by laurels,
Chocolate eggs hidden in foliage.
Unexpected sun drew us outside
To cut grass. Heady with the spilled
Scent of garden we lazed on the patio,
Ate 'do-it-yourself' meals,
Exchanged news between glasses of wine.

This garden ends in a line
Of swaying conifers. It snows.
I build a patio, stone by stone
And see how the walnut tree's
Antlered branches outgrow the house.
From inside: the ring of voices,
The song of blood... Soon
The birds will leave this nest and
Stretch their wings in summer skies.
When the seasons end, they will come again.

Taut wires between telegraph poles
A gathering of swallows.

Endless Sky

The young must learn to fly and I,
Restlessly winged, must wait.

The bright-eyed fledgling at my side
Swerves unsteadily through a rush sky.

Around us fields lie lushly green
And May's white-breasted harbingers

Of light stitch the evening, dart
And flit unseen between wide flourishes

Of oak. With hooded eyes I watch
My shadow float and dream of endless sky.

Skeined Rivers of Dark

I was homeless: you rescued me
Taking me to your stone cottage –
The staggered garden burned
With schumach trees, forgotten apples
Fermented in uncut grass.
We drank tea on the crazy terrace,

The air heavy with bees.

Weeds displaced flowers,
Flowers grew on paths,
Fuchsia squeezed between thorns:
Bruised faces pressed against glass.
Later we walked and let the dogs lead us
Through skeined rivers of dark.

That night we toyed
With sharing the master bed.
'There's one electric blanket,'
You said. You were convincing
Yet I chose the blue room
And woke to a solitary dawn

The sky restless with swallows.

I came, soft on tiptoe to find you find you
Face-down onto pillows,
Limbs aligned. On either side of you
A hound reclined: ears cocked, slit-eyed.
Your smooth shoulders and tousled head
More boy's than man's in sleep.

Still, when we meet I drift on a hairbreadth
That pulls me towards you keeps us apart.

The Eve of May

Clouds, full as wind-blown sails
Pass swiftly and the rain
Is no more than a gesture.

The tide of new-cut grass
Idles and furrows. Unleashed
You are a gun-shot: a streak

Of white. You sight a low-flying
Thrush, accelerate and brake
Skidding through green spray.

She lifts. Leaves you grounded,
All legs and ears and tail:
A trembling exclamation.

The unseen trembling of boughs
Break at each tip. New flesh
Is greedy for light. The chestnut's

Coned candles split sheaths,
The oak anticipates release.
Yesterday it snowed.

Today,
A stab of sunlight, one swallow,
The almond is in blossom.

Isopod

If more people were aware
That on account of its pale blue blood
An isopod is semi-aristocratic and therefore
Entitled to such eccentricities as:

Appearing in forty different forms,
Breathing through its fourteen legs,
Carrying its young in a low-slung pouch
Across its chest and rolling, armadillo-like

Into a tiny perfect ball
At the slightest intrusion, they would
Perhaps refrain from such insulting terms
As: woodlouse, bug or tiggy hog.

Surely those of royal blood
However thin,
Deserve some sort of privacy
And a decent show of respect,
However small.

Attack

A sun-fondled, dove-song Sunday
Is ripped apart.

The sky unfurls, hurls
From its open jaws
Three frenzied magpies:
A black and white whirling alarm.

Outstretched wings – venom-tipped,
Screams to curdle the blood of a witch –
Spiked talons striking air,
Ready to tear to pieces the cat
Slung low on the lawn
Holding a floundering magpie
In a moist, red grip.

White eyed and terrified
The cat unclamps its jaws, backtracks.

'Write A Poem'

'Write a poem,' he said,
'Be as quick as you can
And when you've finished
Put it there on the table!'

He has a special way
Of saying 'there'
That I like.
It reminds me of a day last summer
When we climbed a hill,
The sun hot on our shoulders.
We rested at the top,
Talked as we sat.
I remember the way he said 'hair'.
The same sort of word.
I remember liking that.

(*Writing workshop poem.*)

The Last Time

Do not let the last time be the last time.
We have taken the seasons and made them our own

We have tasted the sharp edge of spring,
Watched April's laser beams probe sodden fields,
Seen daffodils thin buds grow large
And burst in a frenzy of yellow,
Black skeletal trees stir and prick green.
We have felt the late winds grow soft,
The sun's first burst of warmth
Through scudding cloud brush our skin.
We have known the first heartbeat of spring.

Do not the last time be the last time.

We have loved swallow-flecked, wide-eyed summer,
Walked lanes headachy with the spilled scent of flowers,
Seen purple foxgloves strain to overreach
The hedge-tops. We have watched the river idle
Between stones, fingering overhanging boughs.
We have lazed in the splashed shade of the oak
Making dreams. We have heard the thatch tick
And creak and grow silent over us.
We have known the throb of summer.

Do not let the last time be the last time.

We have felt the weight of autumn's gold,
Watched black embers of crows tossed
Over a bonfire of trees, searched snowdrifts
Of leaves for chestnuts, hedgerows for berries
That bleed, staining our fingers, our lips purple.
We have woken to find the river swathed in mist,
The field pebble-dashed with mushrooms,
Leaves like careless confetti drifting.
We have known the slow burn of autumn.

Do not the last time be the last time.

We have witnessed the big striptease of winter,
Seen arthritic limbs of trees unclothed,
Heard the swollen river suck through its teeth.
We have walked, bent double against the saw-edge
Of wind, startled inquisitive bullocks with a gesture,
Sheltered under the fir's black umbrella.

We have made poems while logs burn,
And let the day close.
We have known the low pulse of winter.

Do not let the last be the last time.
We have taken the seasons and made them our own.

Exit

There's no time for tears, she told herself
As she left the campus, passed the chaplaincy centre
Spiralling into customary cloud. One last glimpse
Of mountains and below, the estuary
Shining, shining...

It's ruined by pylons she told herself,
Not to mention Pontins shaped like an ocean liner
Side by side with the nuclear station.
Past the deserted hitching post, the plane leaves
Waving waving...

This is no place tears she reminded herself
As the M6 sucked her south – the back of her yellow car
A rattling tortoise hump of clothes, books and a year's
Collection of *objects trouvés*: sheep's teeth, bones, driftwood
Floating, floating...

Think of the bad times she reminded herself:
The typewriter choked with Tipp-Ex,
Stretched, sleepless nights, dawn strangled by the oak's
Cloaked horny hands. Rain. In three days his plane
For Cairo leaves Heathrow.

It was the cigarette lighter that did it.
The place: a motorway café, just north
Of Birmingham. The flame
Burning, burning …

Fellow passengers stopped momentarily
To stare. Amazed by the sight of a woman
Her face glazed with tears
Learning, learning

Once, at dusk, their russet car crept
Through the Trough of Bowland
Towards Pendle Hill – admiring its jewelled reflection
In the bay below. Then there was the time
They drove to see the sun set at Sunderland Point,

Parked on the beach, they dared the incoming tide
To reach them. A red-setter chased oyster-catchers
Across the bed of reeds. They swung over him,
Black, bat silhouettes – screaming, screaming…

Sea and sky, sky and sea bled.

She walked ahead. 'You can't take that log with you,'
He said – believing her passion for driftwood
Had grown elephantine – when really
She was arranging it as a seat for them
To watch the sun's bald head, crimson and swollen

Falling, falling…

They followed the frayed fringe of beach
Past the grave of a slave who died at the hands
Of the boomerang tide, to a lane between
Fluorescent hedgerows and fields dusty with rabbits –
Their tails white filaments. Her hand lost in his. Safe.

Now he's a name in the flame
Burning, burning…

Christopher

Today I thought about you, vulnerable,
Anti-violence, amidst the violence
Of The Cape. Your letter states
That by comparison the I.R.A.

Play Sunday-school games. Last night
I listened to the tape of you and me
And Peter talking in my room and recalled
The day we walked the Crook o' Lune,

The way the path led through
Garlic-scented woods, amazed with
Bluebells and starred, white anemones,
To the crest of a hill where a curlew

Dragged her wing to lure us from
Her nest. Today, thirty pairs of eyes
Fastened on me. I heard my voice:
'The oak tree thrust it fist.'

My mind slipped back to the oak tree
In the square outside my window –
Darkness blotting the leaves.
On tape – your voice is soft.

It lilts. You speak of your
Recent trip to Greece – the wild herbs
You picked are perfumed still –
And of you fishing in the Wit Els

In Southern Africa. Upstream, you glimpsed
A naked couple, rolling cigarettes.
A drift of marijuana: a dream of peace.
Outside this window – the resident squirrel

Harvests the fruit of a walnut tree.
Wind sifts paper leaves. In the poster
You sent of Table Mountain, armies
Of exotic flowers camouflage the townships.

Among the photographs on my desk is one
Of you, arms outstretched as if to diminish
Distance. Today, I missed you. Today,
I wished you near and safe.

Peninnis

Today, Peninnis is ours:
Yours for nine summers and still
You lose your way and take me
By the wrong route to a promise
Of cool drinks at an imagined place
Overlooking the bay.

We find ourselves wading waist deep
Through bracken, alive with butterflies
Along a track that leads to a sea
Of vibrant blue agapanthus:
A misplaced tropical garden
Walled by Sicilian hedges that
Brush the sky.

And now you run and shout
For the sheer joy of this place
While I, a newcomer, am dumb:
Silent Madonna gazing across
Absurdly turquoise sea
To scattered islands.

Yesterday, we lay among the dunes
Of Saint Agnus and walked knee-deep
Through ice-cold sea to Gugh –
Too impatient to wait
For the receding tide to pave
The way.

On the horizon, Round Island
Lighthouse is white. Last night,
From Tregathenan its red eye
Exploded silently every ten seconds.
The sleek, oiled bay and all
The outside world of boats and quay
And grey stone houses became no more
Than shadows invaded by an image
Of the room. The sepulchred toll
Of the underwater buoy mourned
The loss of life, the loss of day.

We find a hollow in a pink cloud
Of thrift, surrounded by
Huge buttresses of rock –
Unashamedly phallic: a sculptor's
Dream fashioned by wind and wave
And sky.

Gulls wheel and dive:
Indifferent voyeurs with unblinking
Eyes. From a headland
Binoculars scan the rocks for seal
Or shag and find instead two mermaids
On Peninnis.

Canoeing: Ardeche River, France

The road straightens, the sky
Hangs an hour ahead over Monet fields,
Farmhouse roofs shelve red, an endless avenue
Of trees lead to falling horizons.

She wakes to the hum of wheels
Through fields of lavender.
Star-fingered vines gesture to the sun,
Cherries bleed from thickly bedded leaves
And hills climb one by one to the Ardeche.

The descent to Chataingnerai:
Six hundred feet down a steep, white face,
A goat-track zigzags over
Polished rocks and twisted roots
Takes them to a semi-secluded, secret place:

The sun shuttered between white walls,
Dappled shade dances beneath leaves of acacia.

The River Men, oiled and bronze as gods
Know her well – wary of her changing mood
They trace each curve, smooth a path between rocks,
Take the rapids upright in full flood.

On calm stretches they pull together,
Each paddle a spade to dig the water.
The plop and trace of bubbles
Draw half-circles, follow the canoes.

Breeze lifts and cools strands of hair
From her forehead and neck.

The newly ruffled water forms a V-shape
That grows, spans the river, pulls the canoe
In its quickening flow to the rapid's head that grows.
She braces herself for the first ice-cold wave
Leaping upstream:

'Oh my God!' an involuntary cry from within.
From behind. 'Paddle, paddle hard!'

She pits herself against the backward slinging tide,
Plunges the paddle in and in and in,
Presses her feet against the sides,
Angles her body between. Tips headfirst over 'Russia'

– The gleam and rush of water – swings between glazed
Rocks:
– Great fossilised bears standing midstream.

'Keep right! Keep to the right!'
Over a network of white-ribbed currents
To catch the forward fleeing tide, pulled into a flying dream.

'Magic!' he said 'Magic!'
She smiled. The magic grew inside.

High, overhead swallows swing
Between the white walls of the gorge, piping
They melt into the sun. Backstage
A toad sings bass. A trout backflips and is gone.

They pull through sluggish green
To the welcome black of shade.
Lines of heat bend and shine over
The white arc of beach.
Knee-deep in water she watches minnows
Explore her fractured legs, her splayed feet.
He climbs the grey cliff-face to a narrow ledge.
Poised as though to jump he flings himself headfirst
Into a perfect swallow curve, hangs mid-air, mid-way,
Straightens and slips between dark waves.

A pair of dragonflies in an emerald embrace –
Stop and start and stop. A sleek seal head,
A line of bubbles come this way.

Through the chestnut's fan of leaves –
The evening sky, a diamond studded cliché darkens.
Still dressed for the sun they dance
Absorbing each other's heat. Joan Armatrading sings
'Me, myself, I,' backed by a chorus of cicadas.

Fields of sunflowers unfurl to Nimes and beyond
To Marseilles. A mistral has had the ocean by the throat
For five days. It is said that a man committing a grave
Offence
At this time may plead insanity and will be proved innocent.

As the great cobra head rears and sways,
She tucks her board under her and springs, clings
To flying mane, speeds through splintered, beaded ice,
Higher and faster, smiling: a green deluge overhead.

She holds her belly board as a spear, prepares for the next
attack:
Feline, ready to strike, dives through the wall of green glass,
And lunges forward against the water's weight,
Crouches again… beyond the lines of curling white
She turns to face the land.

She seeks anonymity among the beach umbrellas,
Finds a space to stretch, lets the sun have its way.
Through lizard lids she watches the weave of pedlars:
'Beignet, boissons frais, de bonnes glaces.'
The drum of waves. The heaviness of heat…
The Carmargue – fifty kilometres away:
A dream of white horses – the pink afterglow of flamingos
Flushing inland lakes, salt rivers snaking through reeds.

'It's a wasteland. There's nothing to see.' they said.
She let her eyes run over the rows of tents,
The concrete spread. Closed her lids,
Found a wasteland in her head.

In Transit

Selection of poetry written while on overseas postings
in Singapore, Libya, Brunei, Australia, Namibia,
Botswana & the United Arab Emirates.

Singapore

Ang Mo Kui
(Red-haired devil)

I live on an island, fifteen hours
As the swallow flies from home,
On the fifteenth floor of a high-rise
Highly technological block.
They've scooped the hills
Into the sea to make it perfectly flat
for perfectly straight sky-scrapers
to grow side by side. Every day
I dream about horizons.

Don't say we didn't warn you.
It's time to settle. Think
About the children.

My children come out of the sky.
We spend our days on the sea
Learning the rootless language of waves.

There are no seasons here. Daylight
Clocks on, clocks off. All year
Day and night, fans churn sluggish heat.
I've never believed in saunas.
My body grows as soft as the cells
Of my brain. I've lost all perimeters

I sleep to the sound of sucked in rushing
Wind. Guard dogs are howling.
The burglars are so thin they worm
Up rubbish chutes. Silent as cockroach.

The girls like European men for their size
And the colour of their skin.
They walk beneath umbrellas, etiolate
In air-conditioned rooms, dressed for cocktails.
They make perfect wives.
I'm nutmeg brown, I smoke Indonesian
Cigarettes. I taste of cloves.

Yes, I will visit soon,
In the golden flesh, I promise.
England in June. I have lungs again
Skin that fits, stalked nipples.
I move with sprung rhythm, finger the lives
Of friends, laze in overgrown gardens.
I'm amazed at the delicacy of a dog-rose,
Buttercups spilt gold.
Tell me, was the sky always this wide?

I queue for the Summer Exhibition.
A girl is playing a violin. The notes so pure,
I weep. At the British Museum I dream
With Utomara's girl: three aubergines, two hawks
And in the smoke-blue distance Mount Fuji burning.

An inter-city nomad, north to south,
East to west. It's foxgloves I remember
Ten feet high and the way lanes twist and twist
Careless between fields.

On a train to Colombo, we're stacked like cattle.
Sweat runs into my eyes, trickles warm as urine
Down my legs. The women have owl eyes.
I sit on the floor, cross-legged, wheels jarring my bones,
Watching between the alpha legs of a man
At the open door- the bold red sun bouncing
On the sea's edge. At Polonnaruwa I was as high
As the feet of the sleeping Buddha.

The one hundred and twenty-five glides through green
waves.

Believe me, idyllic tropical island
Do not exist. I've seen them all.
Strips of blisterng, talcum sand fringing jungle.
Once I crept inside. At first nothing except
The unnerving shrill of cicadas and deep, dark
Dripping heat. Then I saw a a twelve-foot iguana
Lumbering through fallen leaves and tangle lianas.

La recherche du temps perdu. There are things
I haven't told you. Things I've almost forgotten.
The emerald sea's everything Cousteau dreamed up.
Everything. *Keep your eyes wide!* The purple eye
Of a sea urchin is following me. It flexes
Its wavy fronds as I pass. Strikes.

The boatman hammers the pain
With a piece of rock.
Later, I lie flat on my back, burning.
He applies fresh lime, hammers again.

Travel does not necessarily broaden the mind.
There are tea-leaves between the pages
Of my books. I'm packing seaters. Ignore all rumours
I'm having withdrawal symptoms for mountains.
I'm adjusting the strings of my parachute.

Penthouse Party

She brought her psychoanalyst to the party.
His beautiful, doe-eyed wife
Has an uncontrollable passion for ice-cream.
She's the Mexican Queen in black lace
With a Kiwi accent, juggling her breasts.

The pilot's on his way from San Francisco
Dreaming of my crisp white sheets.
I'm in love with a manic depressive
Who's obsessed with his daughter. I'm hiding
In the jungle, dancing with a whiskered man

I do not care for. The Queen's pressing
Her thighs against an Englishman
Who thinks in French: *l'ardeur de l'amour*;
She hands me a fat black olive disguised
As a grape. I think I'm feeling sick.

She's dancing between the legs
Of intimate strangers and balloons dangling
From creepers like overripe fruit,
Slipping lies into drinks: salt-rimmed glasses
Of tequila, like crushed snow.

The whiskered man's trying to get inside
The hole in my head. I don't speak Hokkein.
He has hooked fingers. He thinks I'm a violin.
Imagine tumbling over and over on the piste
In black lace with the Red Queen! I wish

I were the gecko slipping behind the painting
Of the anorexic Indonesian, floating
Over the neon city. The psychoanalyst,
Slumped across the feet of the reclining Buddha,
Is suffering from stress.

Lichees

Through the open French windows the swimming-pool
Holds the emerald day. She arranges fruit.

A pyramid in a porcelain dish: ornamental gourd,
Snow pears from China, Filipino melons

And on the peak, delicately balanced lichees:
Small grenades. Uniformly subdued Japanese kids

Arrive from school, strip and assault the pool.
Their rapid metallic voices ricochet.

Emerald fragments shatter. Last night
She heard them through the balcony's jungle

Of bougainvilleas and palms. Nearer,
The afternoon's battle rages on. A parakeet

Flashes yellow alarm between eucalyptus leaves
Overhead someone playing Brahms.

She closes the smoked glass doors to listen
Bullets rattle on – takes a lichee

In her hand, squeezes it, imagines herself
Pith-helmeted, crepuscular, armed.

Face to Face

(The British Council, Collyer Quay)

We sat in his office. He talked.
I, switched to guttural response, wondered

How, after years in the tropics,
He remained so pale, so delectably cool

His eyes: just a shade or two
Lighter than the tasteful blue

Of the walls – sunlight painted
The tips of his lashes gold – one long,

Long leg looped across the knee
Of the other swung gently to

And fro – and whether he flew
To England for shirts with sleeves

That reached to his elegant wrists
And how long it would be –

Then we were both on our feet,
His hand warm and firm in my grip.

Welcome to the Circus
(Voice of the Ministry of Education)

Today you're for the trapeze.
You don't like heights,
Have practised juggling all week.
There are too many jugglers.
I see you were late.
The monsoon, you say,
And six people jumped you for a taxi.
Keep on your toes.
Last month as Courtesy.
This month Achievement.
Please note:
We can demote without notice,
Dismiss without reason.
No, you're not free to leave.
Holidays? Mandatory?
Unfortunately, you are deceived.
We allocate at our discretion.
Application in triplicate please.
Form 507.
Alternative to trapeze?
Let me see?
We do need a head for the mouth of the lion.
Position as clown?
Taken, he said, adjusting his frown.

Waiting for Wind

All day we sit on the Casuarina Terrace,
Harnesses within reach, watching
The flag. Sailboards like luminous-winged
Basking seals, litter the beach. Once
We read books and did creative things

With the children. Someone has ordered
The first jug of beer. By noon
The table creaks. The children are under
The rotting platform where the sea
Creeps in, squashing crabs into

Plastic cups. Burs from the casuarina
Bruise your feet. *Has anyone seen Byron?*
I'll swear I saw the leaves on that palm
Stir. Clouds crowd the horizon like
Inflated sheep. Someone's hallucinating.

He's drifting with the current.
When he's out of sight the rescue boat
May look for him. He's looking small.
He's looking sad. The deadly sea snake's
Mouth is so small it can only bite

The loose skin between your finger
And thumb. I'm easing into non-
Slip fingerless gloves. The pilot dips
His silver wings over the ocean.
He's coming home. He's not excited

By dark girls who float up and down
Over the waves in long, soft robes.
He likes me in my yellow harness.
I've told him, over and over,
I'm in a coma. I'm waiting for wind.

Windsurfing

Butterfly wings tilt, huge against the sky.
My Wanderer flutters, pale aquamarine.
Your Swordtail's already in flight.

Sinewed anger keeps your muscles tight,
Fingers locked to the boom you attack
Each humped-back wave, spill

Wind from the sail, spray the water white as if speed
Will exorcise the hate that sets your face
To silence. I follow your broken trail,

Salt spray stings and flies. Sails across
Bows we run in to a palm-flecked beach,
A Polynesian bar where a woman waits:

Unopened novel face down, a half empty bottle
Of vodka. She nurses hate behind dark glasses.
In each lens a sun explodes. A troubadour

Of married love I take my leave.
I'm too well-versed in the glint of knives,
The reek of blood to need new lines.

Butterfly wings, like wilted flowers
Are strewn across the waves.

*(The Wanderer and the Swordtail are Malay butterflies found in
Singapore – noted respectively for drifting and swift flight)*

Water-Bed

They've cut away the lump that grew
Into a breast. Beneath the dressing
A prickly reef fringes an island.
Salt-faced the Chinese surgeon
Heard your plea: '*Save my nipple!*'
Silenced you under a white mask.
Startled eyes fell. You dreamt

You walked on sea. We celebrate
Non-malignant news in the shell
Of my papasan's underwater cushion.
Plump fish nibble and stare.
You've bought flippers and wear
A deep blue shirt unbuttoned
To the waist. Yesterday,
A mast fell from the sky.
You explore my bruise: bigger
Than your makeshift breast. Purple,
Deep as Proserpine's crushed grapes.
We are such stuff as fish
Kiss on. When I die I'll leave you
My sailboard. Deliver me to the waves.

Letters Arrive from Europe

We walked in the woods at Fountainblue.
How you would love it! Crunchy fallen leaves,
The sun – a low bronze disk stealing
Our breadth. We picked wild champignons...

The cathedral spire lifts clear of hills
And winter trees, fronds of mist trace
The River Fal to the sea ...

She dreams winter. Frost fired days,
The air diamante-bright, skin flushed
And bright as a Worcester apple's.

Remembers the slow fall of dusk,
The way Hornby's sway and creak overhead catching
The moon and fleeting cloud in webbed fingers.

She places her thumb on her wrist, feels
The slow pulse tick, the blood sluggish.
Damp heat keeps her lungs limp.

She is closest to herself when she is on the sea:
The bright, wide bay alive with striped triangles,
Indonesia's purple nudging the horizon.

Her sailboard steps over polished waves.
She pulls the sail taut against tugging
Currents, tastes the smell of salt.

A coconut's hairy face passes, lurches
Into the wake. Rainbowed furrows break like ice.

Orange Pippin

Today, I have autumn in my hand
Bought for one dollar fifty
From Cold Storage. It warms
In my fingers, spins green
Globe, flushed marigold – conjures

The tang of orchards, long
Grass, moss-encrusted trees.
Black wellingtons squeak and shine
Along a trail of lop-sided daisies.
Mauve. You drive

Through autumn, pull in amidst
Flurries of snow-falling
Leaves to write: *silver sunlight*
Filtering mist, filigreed cobwebs
Laced between branches.

Your shadow falls on the stilled
Globe. Monsoon clouds gather.
Before the deluge a sudden breeze
Releases a handful of leaves:
Orange – Rust-Red – Gold.

Yen Sang Building

The twenty-fifth floor is where the dentist
Lives. The lift is anti-septic. I'm upside
Down. A masked figure is fiddling with steel.
It catches light. Multiplies. I untie
My fingers. No-one is allowed to see my fear.

My toes are knobbing pale shoes. My skirt
Slips over my knees. My fingers are raw sausages.

There's a four-month foetus in my stomach,
Hard as stone. It will not go away.
The needle's knifing bone. Plastic fingers
Are touching my lips, ferret eyes
Centre on pain. My eyes are telescopic.

At home my dentist's eyes are blue. He's mad
About sailing. Kept only sailing magazines until
I complained then he ordered *Country Life*
And *Vogue*. His waiting-room smells of coffee.

I'm homesick for autumn. Two black holes
For eyes. *Don't close your mouth!*
I'm trying to swallow. I'm trying to pretend
I'm not here. When I was five I refused
To open my mouth. My mother came
And took me away – her lips tight as a purse.

Open! Open wide! I am obedient. When I was six
I was sick on the pavement. I splashed
My mother's shoes. When I die I'll be alone.
Your eyes shift from blue to grey.
Believe me, it is autumn I miss.
The starched assistant is sucking my tongue.

Pool

The pool has swallowed a rectangle of sky
Flawless as a clean-cut jewel.

I stand, toes curled on the tiles.
You lie back, twice my size, your feet

Tucked beneath my heels. On tip-toe I poise
To dive. You somersault, slide beneath me

Stretching to reach the water first.
An explosion of beaded glass and I'm free,

Dolphining through self-made silk tunnels
I surface in a rush of bubbles and lie

Face-down to see you on the pool's bottom
A paler, smaller version, held by

Concentric rings of gold, fractured by
Dancing mosaics. I move me arms in wide, slow

Arcs. Trapped in the underworld you struggle
To follow. I ducktail towards you, touch

Your fingers' tips and lift to light, leave
You: distanced, diminished, gasping for air.

Hieroglyphics

Today, I asked Kong Yuanhau to translate
The Chinese writing on my T-shirt.
Yesterday, I wore it into town.
A Chinese man stopped to stare.
His eyes followed the black weave
From the line of my shoulder
Over my breast's curve to my waist.

From his face I could not tell
If I was declaring love for what I hate,
Hate for what I love,
Advertising coke, a brand of cigarettes
Or myself as a whore.

As Kong Yuanhau translates,
Ancient characters release horizontal words
Dispelling fear:

'From the mountain's peak
A vision of a green and changing land is clear.'

Swallow

I came upon a swallow
Tangled in net: nylon strands
Wound tight about his neck

And wings. Cupped in one hand,
Kitten warm, still as death
He let me cut each biting thread.

Arm outstretched, fingers open:
A puff of thistle-down, then
One flick of his navy wings and

He arrowed to a fleck – turned,
Returned, circled where I stood
Hands shading my eyes. Rooted.

At twilight you spiral to my
Web, testing your wings.
We watch the sky release

Its stars. Last night, I dreamt
We were sucked into the timeless
Whirlwind of the Second Circle.

Today, in bright sunlight,
I see you hovering,
Tapping your fingers. All day

I've been sharpening knives.
Feathers are sprouting from my heels,
A soft breeze stirs in my head.

Australia

(In Transit)

Boxing day. I arrive on your heels.
Gift wrapped. Room 511, striped white
And buttercup yellow, is a steppingstone.
For a week we live on strawberries
And champagne, pace between encroaching walls

Wound tight as caged jaguars. Roots trailing.
Sometimes I slip from the narrow bed
Into ivory silk, sit on the balcony,
Pressed to the shade of a spindly potted palm.
Between concrete blocks the sea rolls out and in.

Once we moved as waves. In this strange place
Familiar selves fade, new angles glint.
New Year's Eve: from a veranda
We watch fireworks explode over Sydney Harbour.
A slow-motion film: magnificent flowers

Unfolding, falling on the falling year.
In a candle-lit room strangers, decked in balloons
Gyrate to scratched rock n' roll. The *nouveau riche*
Thrive like mushrooms in suburbia. *Les uns, les autres.*
Later, we dance and almost find each other.

A new decade, stretched on the beach,
A desert between us. Hot winds strip my skin
Like gum trees' bark. At Alice Springs the night's
As bright as a crystal chandelier. We could diet
In the desert. Catch desert rats. Get drunk on space.

The horizon tilts. The road burns and thrums
Through rushing leaves, dips over skeletal creeks –
Pebble-dashed, root-bound – slows through the neat rows
Of baked suburbia to Room 511.
I'll write from Togo or Brazil, or maybe

From the shade of the *pines parapluies*
In the south of France. I'll become fluent in French.
You'll learn Japanese with a French accent.
We'll perfect communication.
A last spin over the cartwheeling bridge,

The shelled opera house shining
Like Aphrodite newly risen. From the air
Raging bushfires diminish to smouldering
Garden heaps, distance stretches like gold,
Finely spun. The trapped house suffocates.

I wander from room to room between
Sleeping Buddhas, throw open windows
And doors, exchange heat for heat.
The wilting garden, buried in scented leaves
Sinks in darkness and the cicadas' tragic chorus.

Soon the family will return,
Olive-skinned from their Christmas Island.
Lit with smiles. Open armed.
Face-to-face with a humming fan I drift
Towards sleep. Rehearse departures.

Thailand

(Boiling Eggs)

The road from Chiang Mai
Chokes in red dust,
Forests burst into flame as we pass.
Beside a hot stream,
Steaming like an overheated bath
We bargain with tourist-wise kids.
Market prices. Eggs for lunch.

I squat by a mud-hole,
Sun clamped to my back, dangling
Dancing eggs in a fishing-net
Water spits like hot fat –
And think of you
Cutting fingers of buttered toast
To dip into perfectly timed yolk.

Sri Lanka

(The Blue Elephant: Colombo)

At the Blue Elephant
Disco – lights slice and probe
the mating dance of nubile girls.

Sneakered youths, cuffs rolled,
Lose their cool, pull
Gyrating hips to hips, breasts

To muscled chests. Hands close
On the rhythmic roll of apple-buttocks.
The girls' wide-awake eyes

Search darkened alcoves
For more elusive prizes, size up
Paunching males who hold

The bar upright: stiff drinks
Wet their lips, cigarettes
Smoulder between itching fingers.

Libya

(Desert Rose)

Released from the thrumming heart
Of the Sahara, the Ghibli's hot breadth scours
Pavements where dark men brewing tea crouch
And mutter. Rumours of an attempted coup

Glow like hot coals. It is said that Skanska -
The only oasis in this desert – has been raided.
Raped wine vats gape like cavities
From trees uprooted in a gale. The owner's

Under house arrest. Her gun-running days
For Gaddafi erased. They say, her partner's
Revolutionary ways have been paid for
In blood. Today, I slipped past the guard

Into Skanska. Only the pregnant camel stirred.
She sifted through rotten food,
Stared blankly. At my feet
A severed sheep's head buzzed with flies.

Sleek and alert as a desert rat
Gaddafi moves camp from day to day.
The media's strangled silence gurgles.
Still I write postcards as if you receive them.
Only a desert rose can survive this heat,
The abrasive, murmuring wind.
They've had my passport for two months now.
I've heard that the borders are closed.

(*Skanska: ex-pat club*)

The Only Eagle

After months of silence
The sky roared. Startled as Guernica
The whole of Brega stands shading their eyes,
Watching you carve perfect circles in the sky.

Feathered plumes dissolve into blue,
The jolted sun spills crimson onto blossoming cloud.
Had you summoned Venus herself
You could not have conjured such a backdrop

For this debut. I, too was mesmerised:
As wing-tips tilted your soar once more
– The only eagle in the desert sky.
That evening, still winged, in collar and tie

You arrive late. Partygoers gather as moths to a light.
They salute you: saviour of the 'hell run through desert'.
Deep into the night we celebrate
The opening of the star-strung, tremulous sky.

(*Brega: oil company compound*)

Borneo: Brunei

(First Dive: Rig 21)

There are crocodiles in the Belait River;
Dolphins rise from the South China Sea;
A black squall from Sumatra
Tosses the dive-boat like a leaf.
Strapped to my iron lung,
I follow the Moonman, topple
Backwards between flooded

Pylons. They stagger and lean
Like storm-tossed trees. I drop
Feet-first, skull tight as a drum.
Pain is Red. A stream of bubbles
Bleeding from my head. *Ascend*
To ease pain. Never exceed
The rate of ascending bubbles!

In this muffled womb my thrumming head
Amplifies umbilical, laboured breath.
I hover. Fall. *Moonman wait!*
I want to fly. We lie face-down
– Free-falling parachutists
With webbed feet – peer through
Mottled haze at puffballs

Stuck to coral trees and waving tentacles
Disguised as fronds. I reach for blue
Anemones. Moondust crumbles
In my hand. A tugging current tips me
Fins-over-head. Moonman's nursing
A wriggling octopus with luminous spots,
Plump as an overfed baby.

At the third Stage a giant turtle's trying
To sleep. *The sand shark is harmless.*
Last week we found one stranded,
A sweet expression on its face, the spine
On its dorsal fin as fine as a hypodermic needle.
A violent punch on the nose

Of an attacking shark may dissuade it
From pressing further... sea snakes
Should not be provoked. My knife's strapped
To my shin. Striped fish, large and flat
As dinner plates have grim faces.
A tuna trundles past. Tufts of floating
Thistle-down have legs, My pressure gauge
Nudges red. Above my head

A pyramid of silver fish
Shiver like a frosted Christmas tree.
I'm Lazarus, wings on my feet,
Reaching for grey light that sifts
Through billowing curtains. They fall
To pieces in my grasp. My head bursts free.
Mouth full of iron. Blood in my mask.

Bootlegging

We dine at the Mumong Hilton:
Fresh-baked python – strong as overripe fish,
Flat forbidden beer from a cracked teapot.
A mouthful of bones. Darkness strangles
The jungle, follows the Trooper's lights
Along the logging trail to the log-
Strewn beach where my white bungalow

Basks in the fallen sun's rosy glow.
We finish the bootlegged gin, play
Gary Moore's *Midnight Blues* till moth-winged
Walls vibrate. The sea's crazy to come in,
Throws fistfuls of spray at the windows.
A Chinese firecracker explodes. The cloud-stacked
Jungle's having its nightly firework display.

Ibans sniff religious police on the wind, bury
Their tuak in snake-proof vats. Fat Soon's
Supplies have dwindled to two litre flagons
Of Japanese Dragon Vomit. Tomorrow
We'll sail across the border to Miri,
Risk Gadong jail, fill the hold. Dust from Pinatubo
Veils the moon, covers our tracks like snow.

(Ibans – Dayak people)

Hobie-Cat Sunday

A late start to the blood-red strains
Of Bruch's violin concerto: bacon, eggs,
Proper coffee – one eye on the casuarinas
Willing them to bend – then to the boat shed.
We heave the Hobie onto a trolley,

Lug her to the beach: a handicapped maiden aunt.
Dressed and afloat she's a nubile queen.
Wind in her lungs she sings: deep-throated monotone –
Plaintive as the attenuated notes from a violin –
Takes us flying till your trapeze-line twangs apart.

You lean on air, cling to the tiller. It snaps:
A twig in your hand. Baton aloft you drop
Into a hole in the South China Sea, catapult me
Through cart-wheeling rigging. Trapped below
Between taut strings I feel my way to air, hold

Bleeding arms like trophies. *Get on!* you yell.
Torpedoing towards me. *Shark!* We flounder
Onto the sideways hull, haul the Hobie to her feet.
She tosses her head, streaks for the beach,
Sails thrumming. The tip of a silver wing slices waves

Deft as a hot knife through ice-cream.
Blood, like red rain in the wind.

Night-Watch: Star of Siam

I expected stars, sails full-blown
Against moonscape sky, waves lapping
Not this shouldering into the jaws
Of the South China Sea. Sails stowed,
Engine full throttle, we grapple wind-
Backed waves, lunge into heaving black.
Your hands knot on the wheel, eyes shift
From compass to unchartered furrows.
Victora Harbour lights have been doused
Long since. The next light's on Jahat Shoals –

A night-watch away. Amateur trapeze artist
I slither the galley steps, wedge myself
At forty-five degrees before the swaying cooker,
Shed flaring matchheads like distress signals
Till blue flames seize and bloom – orange.
The kettle swings and steams. A frenzied wrist-
Flick flings a cockroach from my hand.
Sweat drips from my chin, trickles
Between my breasts. In the forward cabin
The last watch sprawl open-mouthed:

Battle-field dead in a shroud of sails.
The labouring engine judders. Cuts out.
All hands and knees below deck. My hands
Fixed on the wheel, helpless in the hands
Of the gods of wind and sea. A fishing boat's
Bleary eye's the only star to steer by.
Bled and coaxed the engine revives.
We sip tea, imagine east: the hint of pink
On cloud – dead-reckon where morning's knife-
Edge will prize the pall of sky from sea.

God's Law

They deported Omar for sleeping with his Christian wife.
Raided his house in the night.

The next night you wake me;
Say you're being followed – not to be surprised
If they batter the door, throw you in jail.
They've bull-dozed the Chinese warehouse,
Smashed every bottle. 'It's God's Law!'

All night you sit like a Chinese Buddha swigging illicit beer.
'There'll be none there,' you say.
'Imagine the mess they'll make of my white back
With rattan. They'll love that. Urizen's in control.'

In the days that follow, I keep the bolt on the door,
The shutters closed. It's the season for divine retribution.
In the aftermath of Pinatubo's fiery mission
Typhoon Seth's maddened eye unleashes
Its fury. Monsoon clouds gather and roll.

The frenzied ocean thrashes this coast with logs
From the Baram. Among the debris, a fragile shell:
Nacreous butterfly wing the size of my palm.
Pale survivor of Neptune's dark undertow.

I take it to show you – find the place anchored
In silence and know you have gone – hot-footing
Across swampland and two stagnant rivers
To the border. Kalimantan's inferno of blazing forests scar
To the backbone. A pillar of cloud obscures the sun.

(Urizen: A Godlike figure personifying reason & law)

Sharjah: United Arab Emirates

Khor Fakkan

He left for Kathmandu, leaving her
A box of Cribari Burgundy, his mattress
And bedroll for comfort and protection from rats
In the villa at Khor Fakkan. She wondered
If diving in the Arabian Sea was worth the risk
Of Leptospirosis? Just thinking about the list
Of symptoms made her feverish.

More like a cowshed than a villa
She thought, as she swept straw and rat droppings
Into the garden: a wilderness of sawtooth palms
And banana plantains inhabited by chickens and goats.
She watched a rat test its footing on a rope,
Skitter towards a large hole.

A moonlight dive – mesmerised
By psychedelic ripples – streams of liquid silver slipping
Across the ocean floor. Looking up she watched her breath:
A cascade of silver-coated, expanding bubbles
Rushing towards the moon.

That night she pulled the bedroll tight about her,
Dreamed of rats with purple teeth.
Row upon row of purple mountains rise
From the desert floor: jagged rock pinnacles,
Bare as bone picked clean – an impenetrable gleaming
Fortress.

Martini Rocks: an underwater cathedral of pinnacles
And spires decked out in soft corals of purple and lime-
green.
Like a manic preacher a moray eel opens and closes its jaws
In silent admonition: with a flourish, unfolds like a silken
Ribbon.
A dithering pipe-fish hesitates between congregating shoals
And a procession of banner fish. A nonchalant turtle passes.

At Dibba, fishermen place baby sharks
In rows upon the quay – sad mouths uppermost.
A heap of parrot fish: glazed eyes in a sheen of blue,
Lips parted over tightly closed beaks.
Along the road the miniature mosque's white turrets
Curl like whipped cream – a spider-web window
In each wall. Honey-coloured sun
Through a screen of trees, an ancient fort.

As she leaves the chain of polished mountains,
The bald sun hanging in its scrubbed, blue dome
She thinks of him in the verdant Himalayas
Crowned with autumnal gold – snow-capped peaks –
Sun emerging – red – from turbulent cloud,
Crisp leaves falling – returns to the black tarmac road
Snaking behind naked dunes: the aching emptiness of
Absence.

Also by Adrienne Brady

Non-fiction

Kiss The Hand You Cannot Sever
Melrose Books

Way South of Wahiba Sands
Austin Macauley Publishers

Danger Zones & Pleasure Zones
Austin Macauley Publishers

On the Trail of Saint Paul
Austin Macauley Publishers

Poetry Anthology - contributions
Quintet - Staple UK

From Then... Till Now
Poetry Press, USA

Basic English Series, Poetry 2
Go and Open The Door, Poetry 3
Macmillan Education - UK & Australia

Let Me Be Me - a Junior anthology of poetry
Macmillan, Swaziland

Summer Comes Barefoot Now
Editor EPB, Singapore
Magazine Contributions include:
The Spectator
Poetry Review, Wessex Traveller,
Property World, Dubai

Success as an international prize-winning poet led to an
entry in the
International Who's Who Poets Encyclopaedia

British Library - PLR
Kiss the hand You Cannot Sever…
Way South of Wahiba Sands…
Danger Zones & Pleasure Zones…